This Book Belongs To

____

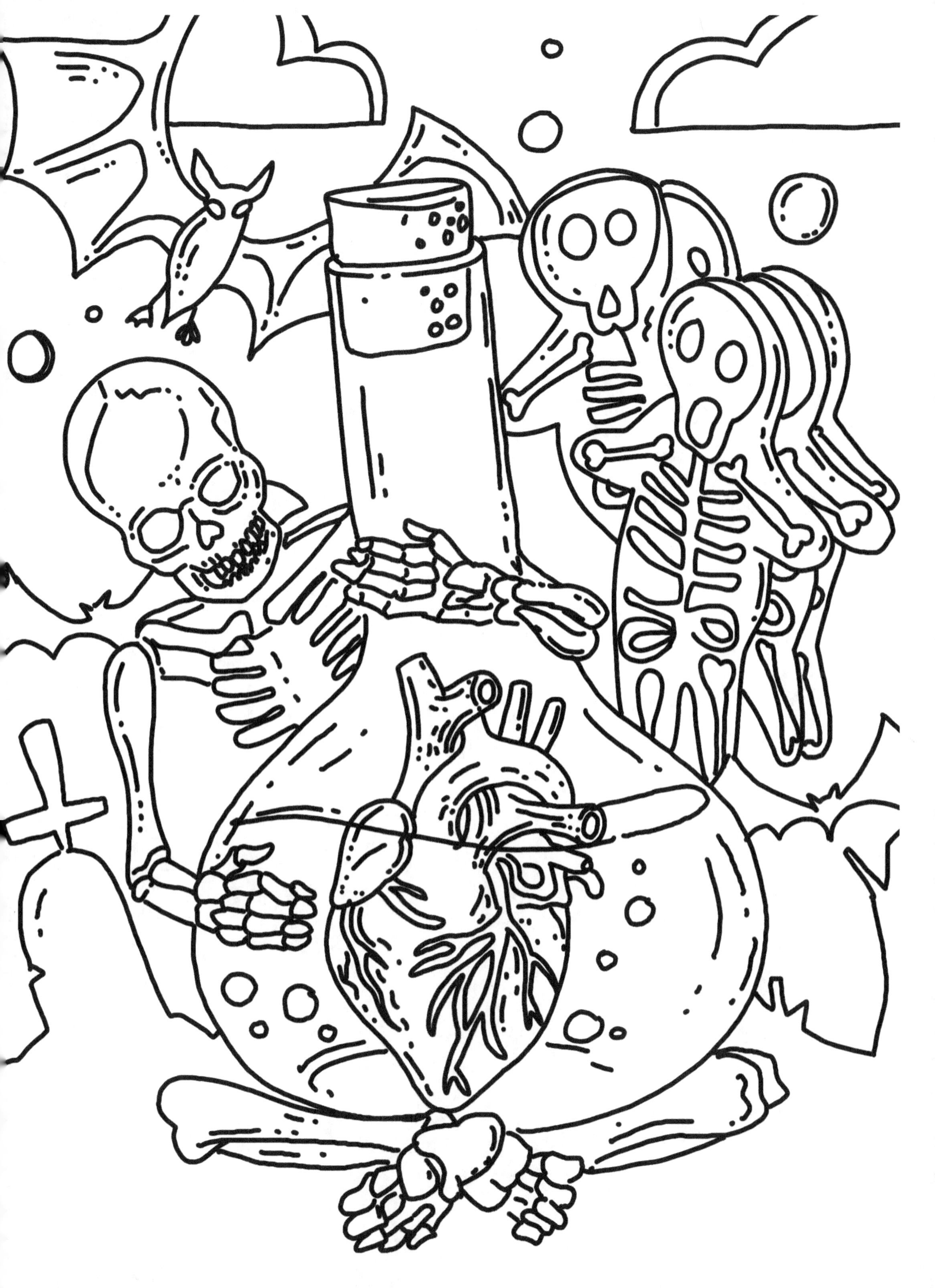

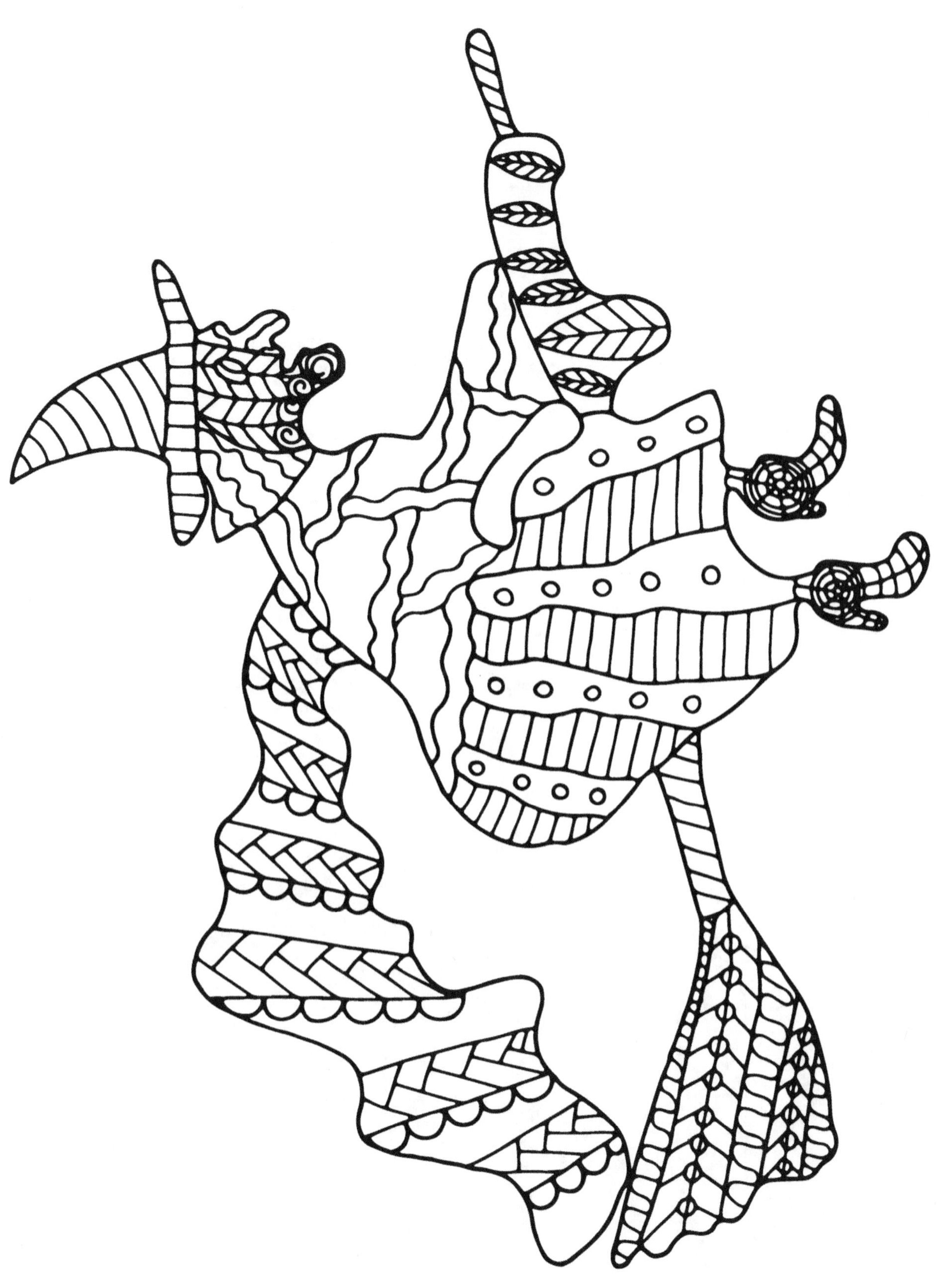

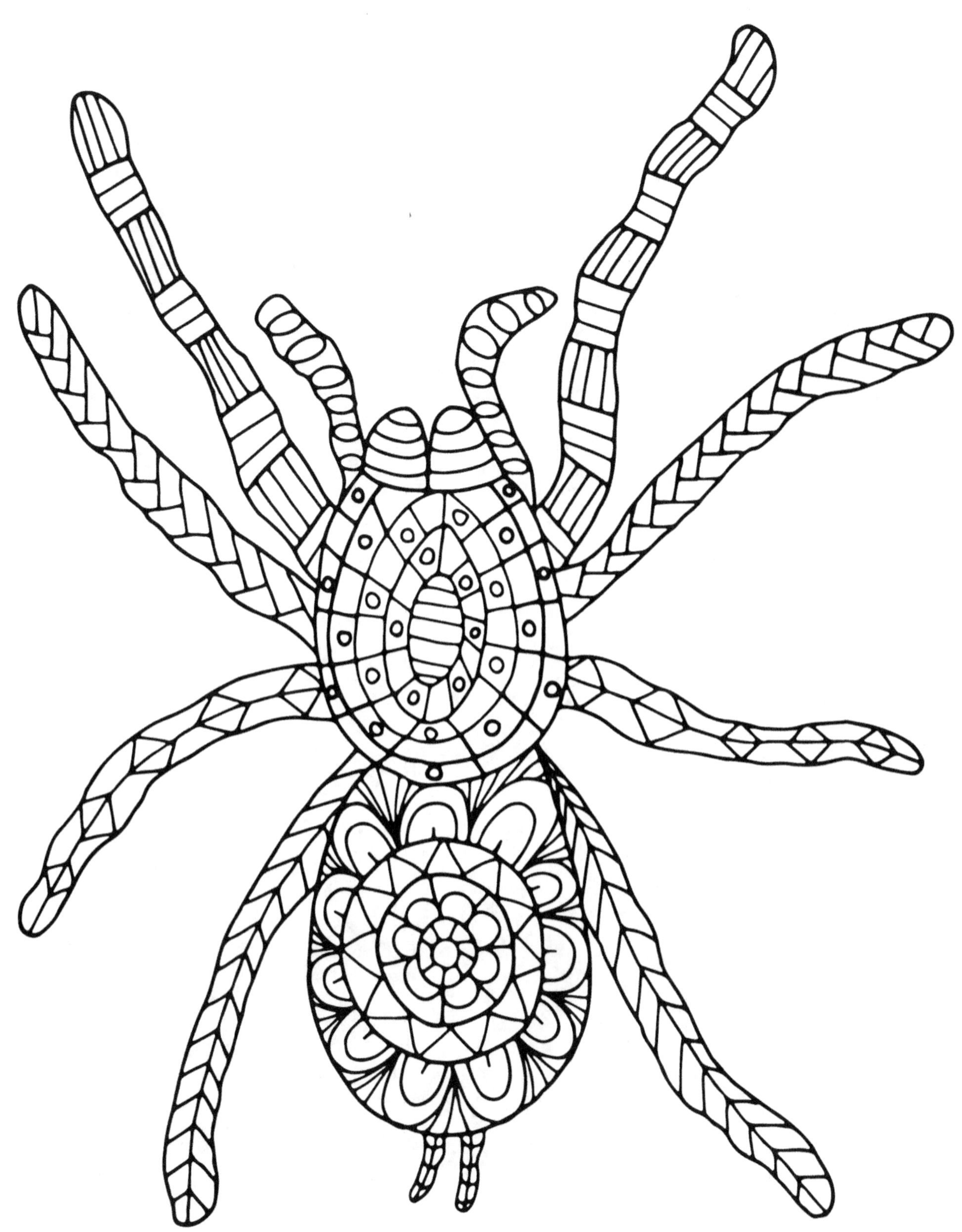

JOY

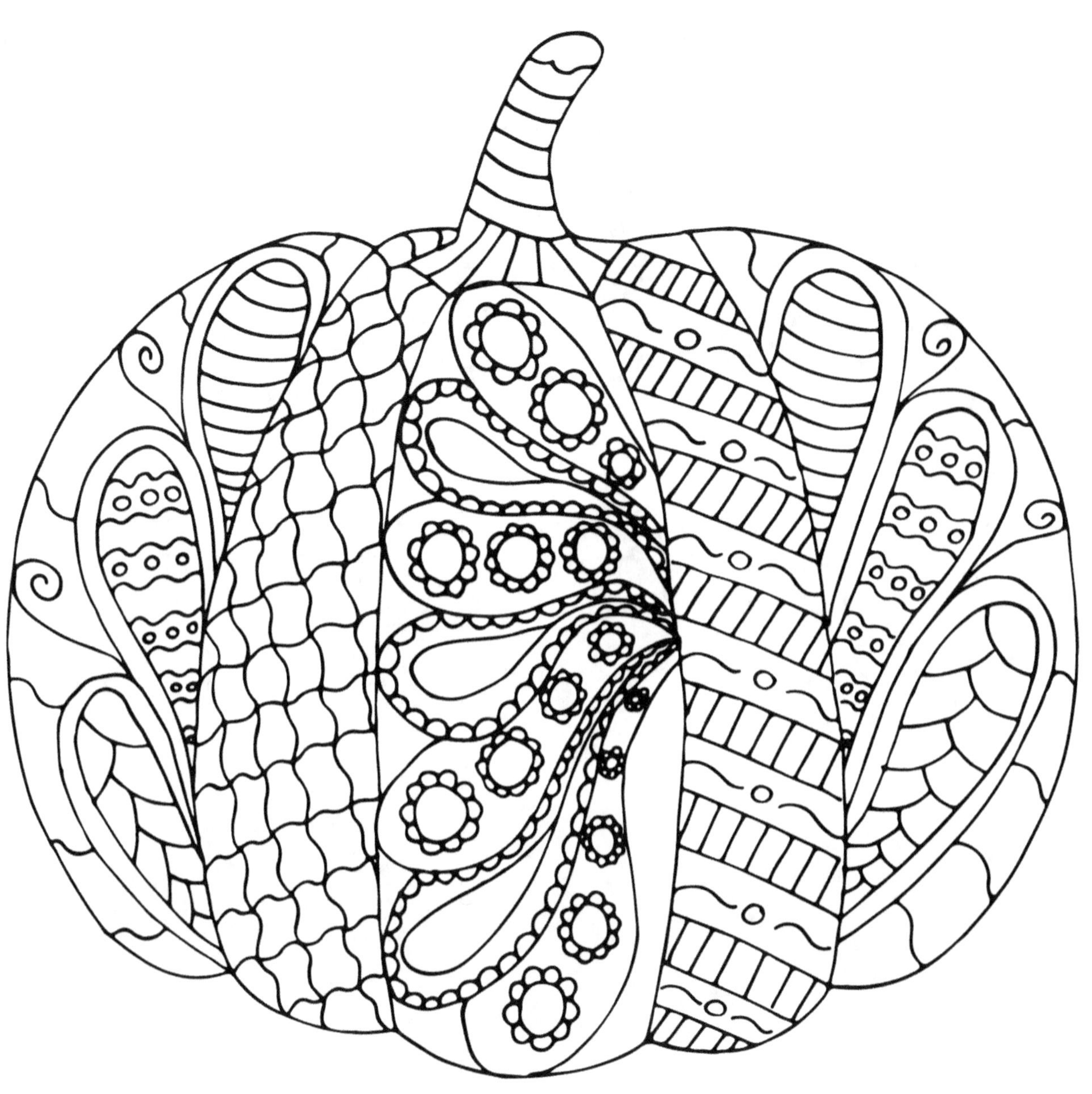

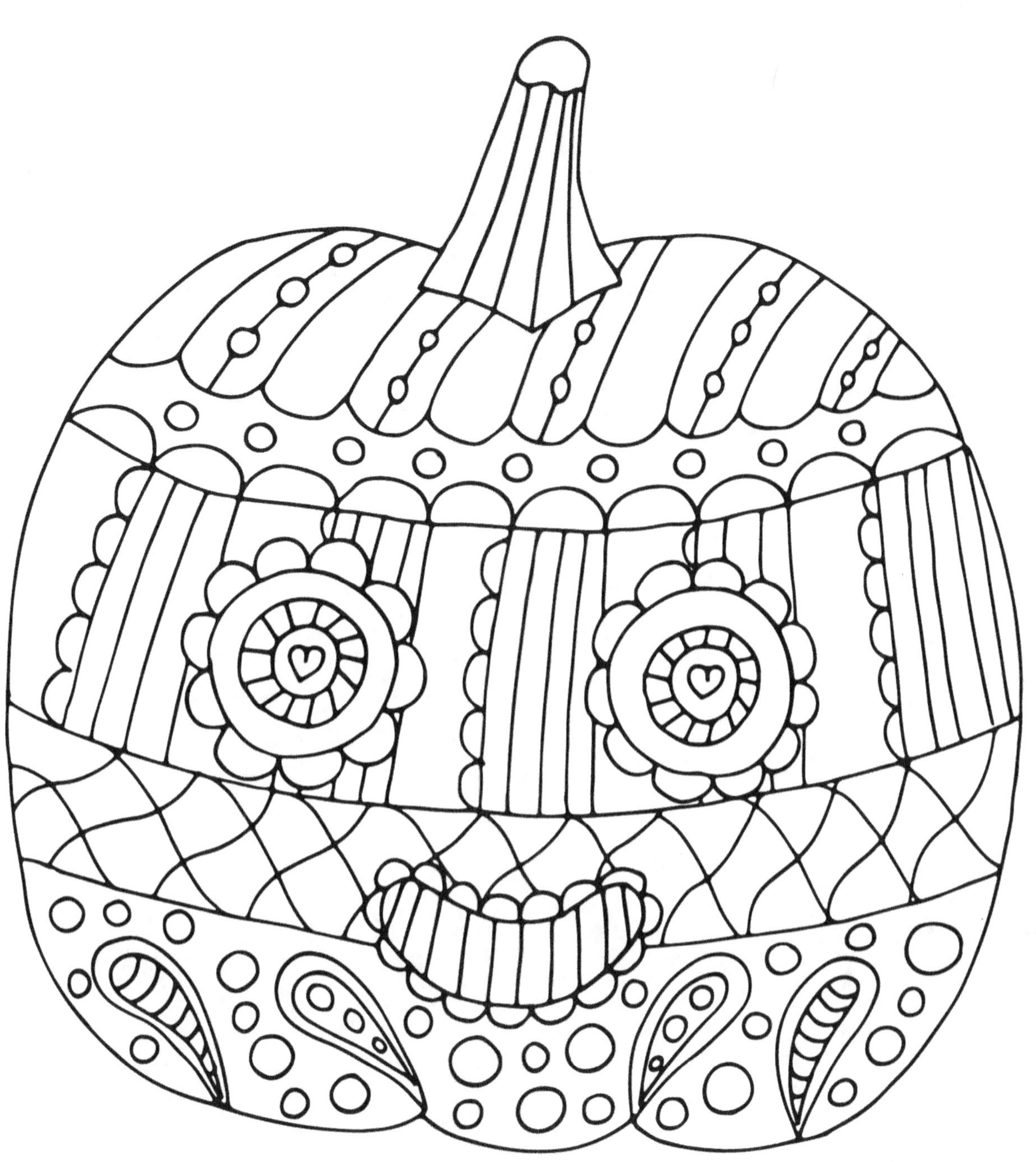

HAPPY
HALLOWEEN

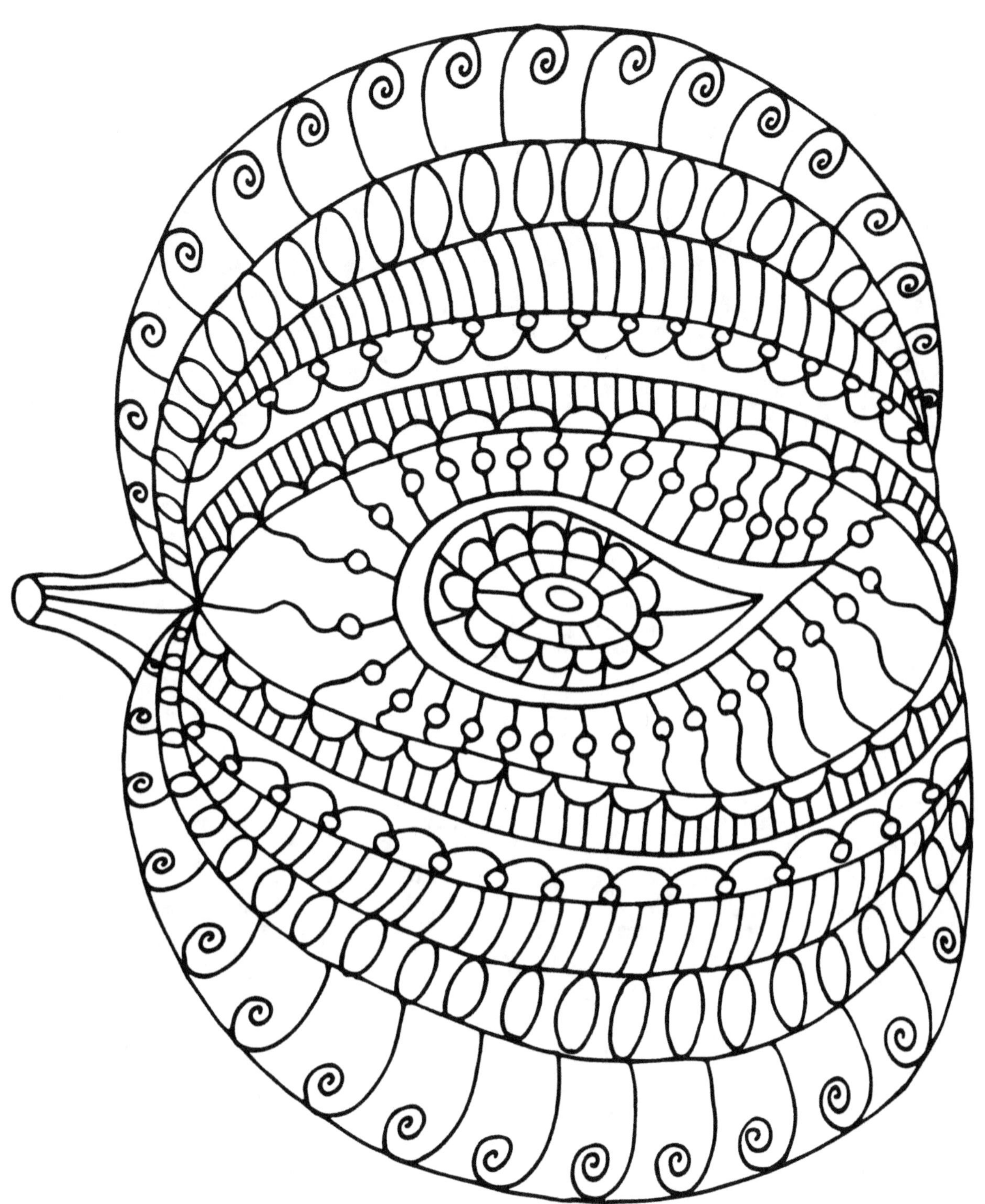

EYE
of
NEWT

Zombie Crossing

HALLOWEEN
PARTY
CREW

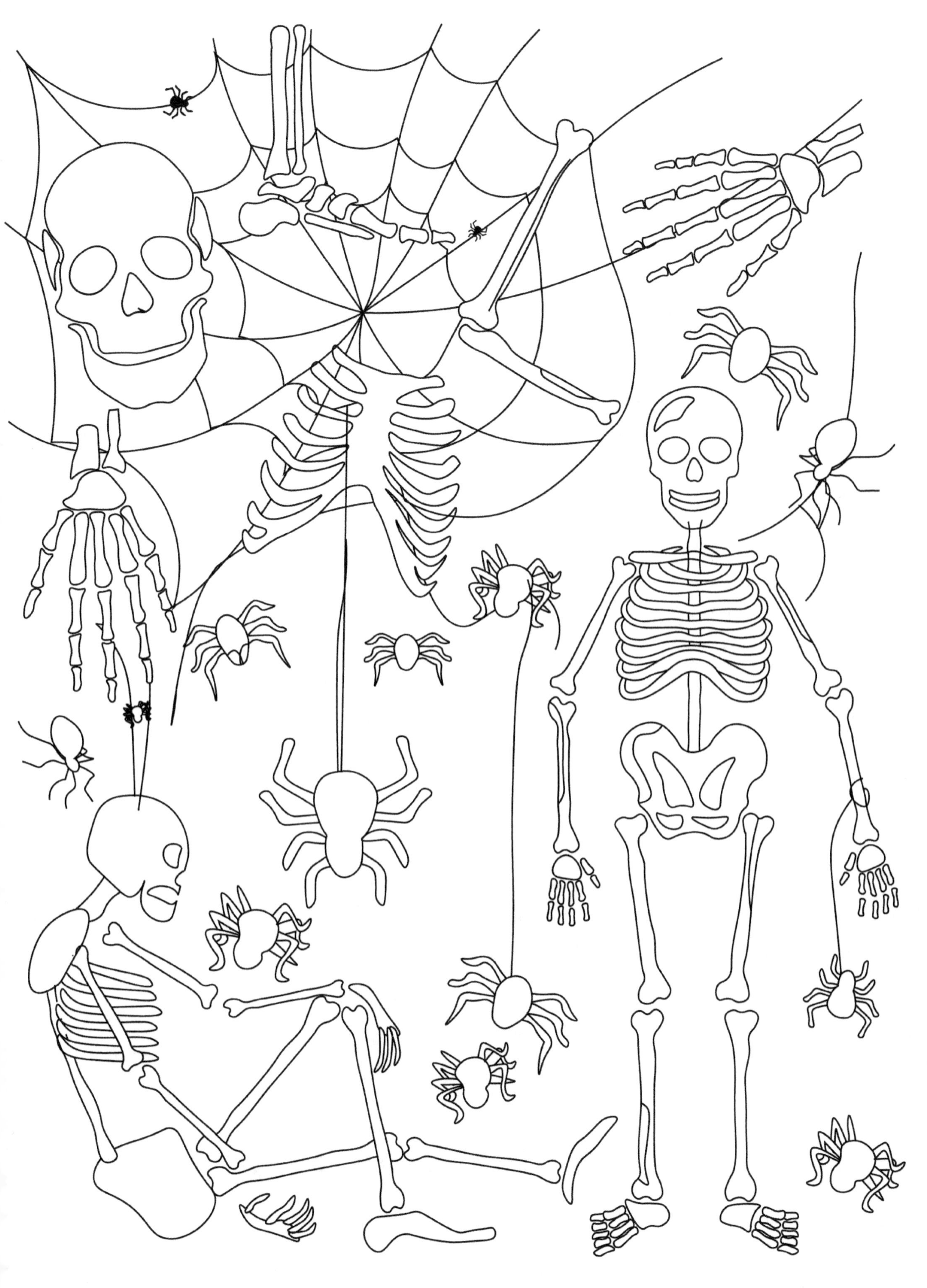

THANK YOU VERY MUCH